반려동물 기초 생활영어

Basic life English for Pets

반려동물 기초 생활영어

이원봉 저

동문사

인사말

반려동물을 사랑하는 사람으로서 반려동물에 대해 공부하는 것에 관심이 있는 학생들을 위해 이 기초적인 영어책을 발표하게 되어 기쁩니다. 반려동물은 우리 삶의 필수적인 부분이 되었고 그들과 효과적으로 의사소통하는 방법을 이해하는 것이 중요하다고 생각합니다.

이 책에서는 영어에 대한 기본적인 이해를 가지고 있지만, 특히 반려동물 관리의 맥락에서 언어 능력을 향상시키고자 하는 학생들의 요구를 염두에 두고 설계되었습니다. 이 책에서 다루는 자료는 간단하지만 유익하며, 학생들이 반려동물 보호자 그리고 반려동물 관리 분야의 다른 전문가들과 의사소통하는 데 필요한 필수적인 어휘와 문법을 갖추는 것을 목표로 합니다.

이 책에서는 일반적인 반려동물 품종, 반려동물 관리, 펫매너, 그리고 동물학 용어와 같은 주제를 다루면서 여러 단원으로 나뉩니다. 각 단원에는 본문에서 다루는 내용을 강화하고 학생들이 실제 상황에서 언어를 효과적으로 사용할 수 있도록 하는 연습과 활동이 포함되어 있습니다.

이 책이 반려동물에 대한 열정과 이 분야의 영어 실력 향상을 바라는 학생들에게 소중한 자료가 되기를 바랍니다. 이 책의 완성을 위해 전문성과 지식을 제공해주신 반려동물 관련 훈련사, 미용사 그리고 반려동물 돌봄 분야의 전문가 여러분께 감사드립니다.

행복한 배움 위하여!

2024. 1.

이 원 봉

차례 CONTENTS

Chapter 06 About pet beauty Ⅲ -Describe your pet's beauty in five areas: Exercise, Breeding

Chapter 07 About pet beauty Ⅳ -Describe your pet's beauty in five areas: Personality

Chapter 08 Dog Training Ⅰ

Chapter 09 Dog Training II

Chapter 10 About the manners of dogs I

Chapter 11 About the manners of dogs II

Chapter 01

Companion animal and humans

1. Word Preview

- **relationship**

Despite their differences, Mary and her brother share a strong and supportive **relationship**.

① 친족 관계, 연고 관계 ② 관계, 관련

- **unique**

Your choice of clothes and accessories can be a reflection of your **unique** personality.

① 유일한, 하나밖에 없는, 독특한

- **domesticate**

Dogs have been **domesticated** for thousands of years. They live with humans as loyal companions.

① 동물 따위를 길들이다 ② 가정에 익숙하게 하다

- **protector**

Maria always makes sure to apply sun **protectors** like sunscreen and wear a hat when spending a day at the beach to avoid sunburn.

① 보호자, 옹호자, 방어자 ② 보호 장치, 안전 장치

- **loyalty**

True friends show **loyalty** by standing by each other, offering support during tough times, and celebrating successes together.

① 충의, 충절 ② 충성, 성실, 충실

- **rescue**

A firefighter **rescues** a child from an apartment fire.

① 구조하다, 구하다

- **therapy**

After injuring his knee playing soccer, John underwent physical **therapy** to regain strength and flexibility.

① 치료, 치료법

- **detect**

The smoke **detecting** alarm in the kitchen immediately went off when it sensed the slightest hint of smoke, alerting the family to a potential fire.

① 발견하다 ② 간파하다, 탐지(감지)하다

- **disability**

Mike uses a wheelchair as an assistive device to help him move around easily, showcasing how technology supports individuals with mobility **disabilities**.

① 무능한, 불구적인, 장애가 있는

- **mutually**

The two companies entered into a **mutually** beneficial agreement, where both parties gained advantages and prospered in their collaboration.

① 상호 배타적인

2. Useful Expression

① Jay and Mike have a great **relationship**. They enjoy spending time together, sharing jokes, and supporting each other

② A fingerprint is a **unique** identifier for each individual. No two people have the exact same pattern of ridges and whorls, making it a distinct and personal characteristic.

③ Cows, chickens, and pigs are common **domesticated** animals on farms.

④ To keep important papers safe, Sam used plastic sheet **protectors** in his binder to prevent them from getting damaged or wrinkled.

⑤ In families, **loyalty** means always being there for each other, helping out, and caring about one another.

⑥ The brave firefighters worked together to **rescue** the family trapped inside the burning house.

⑦ Feeling stressed, Mark decided to take a walk in the park for some nature **therapy**, finding peace and calm amidst the trees and fresh air.

⑧ Tom enjoys spending his weekends metal **detecting** in the park, hoping to find hidden treasures buried beneath the soil.

⑨ The neighborhood is known for its supportive community, where residents come together to help each other, especially those with **disabilities**, ensuring everyone feels included.

⑩ After a thorough discussion, the group reached a **mutually** agreed decision on the project timeline.

3. Reading

The **relationship** between dogs and humans is **unique** and has evolved over thousands of years. Dogs were first **domesticated** from wolves over 15,000 years ago, and since then, they have played an important role in human society, serving as companions, **protectors**, and helpers in various tasks.

For many people, dogs are much more than pets; they are family members and beloved companions. Dogs offer unconditional love, companionship, and **loyalty,** and their presence can have a positive impact on human physical and mental health.

Dogs also play an important role in many professions, such as law enforcement, search and **rescue**, and **therapy**. They are highly trainable and can be taught to perform a variety of tasks, from **detecting** drugs and explosives to assisting people with **disabilities**.

The relationship between dogs and humans is a **mutually** beneficial one, with both species offering each other companionship, protection, and support.

4. Language Practice

Complete the sentences using a word from the box.

• relationship	• unique
• domesticated	• protectors
• loyalty	• rescue
• therapy	• detecting
• disabilities	• mutually

1) Suzie found relief from stress and anxiety through art ( ), using painting and drawing as a creative outlet for self-expression.

2) Snowflakes are ( ). If you look closely, you'll see each one has its own special pattern of ice crystals

3) The teacher learned basic sign language to communicate with a student who has hearing ( ).

4) In a healthy friendship, it's essential to have a ( ) respectful relationship where both friends value and appreciate each other's opinions and feelings.

5) The kids put on their raincoats and carried umbrellas as (　　　　　) to stay dry while walking to school in the pouring rain.

6) Lisa is skilled at (　　　　　) emotions in others; she can easily tell when her friends are happy, sad, or in need of support just by observing their expressions.

7) (　　　　　) at school is when classmates stick together, share secrets, and support each other in good times and bad.

8) A positive (　　　　　) between teachers and students is important for a productive learning environment.

9) Cows are (　　　　　) by farmers for various purposes, such as providing milk, eggs, and meat.

10) The local animal shelter is dedicated to animal (　　　　　), providing care and finding loving homes for abandoned pets.

5. Some General Facts about Dogs

- Dogs are social animals and they form strong bonds with their owners and other dogs.

- Dogs are pack animals and they have a hierarchy within their pack that they follow.

- Dogs have a highly developed sense of smell, which they use to explore their environment and communicate with other dogs.

- Dogs have an innate desire to please their owners and respond well to positive reinforcement training.

- Dogs have a variety of vocalizations, including barking, growling, and whining, which they use to communicate their emotions and intentions.

- Dogs are domesticated mammals that belong to the Canidae family.
- Dogs are social animals and thrive on human companionship.
- They also have a natural instinct to hunt and explore.
- It's important to pay attention to a dog's body language.
- Dogs are intelligent, social, and loyal animals that make great companions.

6. Practical English

Write the following in English

Last First	RM No.
Name : With :	Arr Date :
Resident address:	Dep Date :
	Rate :
Tel : Home : ____ Firm : ____ Mobilephone : ____	Room Type :
Passport No. :	No. of Guests :
Date of Birth :	
Car Licence :	
Method of Payment :	Nationality :

<table>
<tr><td rowspan="2">Check out time is 12:00 noon.
Safety deposit boxes are available at the Front Office cashiers.
Kindly note that the hotel does not accept responsibility for valuable items left in the rooms.

Guest Signature ____________</td><td>Clerk :</td></tr>
<tr><td>Remark:
※ Method of Reservation
1) Internet hotel home-page (　)
2) News paper (　)
3) News letter published from hotel (　)
4) friends or acquaintances(　)
5) News release (　)
6) Etc　(　　　)</td></tr>
</table>

Chapter 02

A General understanding of dogs

1. Word Preview

• descend	• breed
• trait	• thrive
• affection	• instinct
• explore	• intelligent
• bond	• furry

• descend

The colorful kite slowly **descended** to the ground after the kids had so much fun flying it.

① 전래한, 유래한

• breed

Dogs have different socialization needs depending on their age, **breed**, and temperament.

① (새끼를) 낳다 ② 기르다; 양육하다; 가르치다

• trait

My friend Emily has many positive **traits**. She is always kind, helpful, and never forgets to share her toys with others."

① 특색, 특성, 특징, 버릇; 얼굴 생김새, 모습

- **thrive**

We planted a sunflower seed in class, and it started to **thrive**. It grew tall and its bright yellow petals opened up beautifully.

① 번창하다, 번영하다; 성공하다; 부자가 되다; 행운에 젖다

- **affection**

My cat shows **affection** by purring and rubbing against my legs when I come home. It makes me feel loved!

① 애정, 호의, 애착, 연모

- **instinct**

Birds have the **instinct** to build nests to keep their eggs safe. It's amazing how they know what to do without anyone teaching them.

① 본능, 직관, 육감, 직감 ② 천성, 천분

- **explore**

Dogs have a highly developed sense of smell, which they use to **explore** their environment and communicate with other dogs.

① 탐험[답사]하다 ② 탐구하다, 조사하다

• intelligent

My friend Suzy is really **intelligent**. She always helps me with my homework and knows the answers to tough questions in class.

① 지적인, 지성을 갖춘, 지능이 있는, 이해력이 뛰어난, 영리한

• bond

Dogs are social animals and they form strong **bonds** with their owners and other dogs.

① 묶는 것; 속박, 구속; 굴레, 유대, 맺음, 인연; 결속, 결합력 ② 약정, 계약, 맹약; 동맹, 연맹 ③ 담보를 넣다

• furry

My family adopted a furry kitten from the animal shelter. It has soft, **furry** fur and loves to curl up on my lap.

① 모피(제)의; 모피로 덮인, 모피를 걸친

2. Useful Expression

① The colorful kite slowly **descended** to the ground after the kids had so much fun flying it.

② Suzy is interested in gardening. She grows a special **breed** of flowers in her backyard, and they bloom in different colors.

③ When we talk about superheroes, we discuss their special **traits** like bravery, kindness, and the ability to help others.

④ In our garden, the tomatoes seem to **thrive** with lots of sunlight and water. They're growing big and red

⑤ When we adopted our puppy, it quickly developed **affection** for us. It wags its tail and licks our faces to show how happy it is.

⑥ In the wild, animals use their **instinct** to find food and avoid danger. It's like a built-in guide that helps them survive in their environment.

⑦ During our school nature walk, we got to **explore** the forest and find interesting bugs and plants. It was so exciting to discover new things!

⑧ During our group project, we were glad to have an **intelligent** team member who came up with great ideas and solutions.

⑨ Best friends share a special **bond**. They laugh together, play together, and always help each other when needed.

⑩ During show-and-tell, Jake brought his **furry** hamster to class. Everyone was excited to see the tiny, fluffy creature

3. Reading

Dogs are domesticated mammals that belong to the Canidae family. They are **descended** from wolves and were likely first domesticated by humans around 15,000 years ago. They come in many different **breeds**, each with their own unique characteristics and **traits**. Some breeds are better suited to certain lifestyles or tasks than others.

Dogs are social animals and **thrive** on human companionship. They are known for their loyalty and **affection** towards their owners. They have a highly developed sense of smell, hearing, and sight. They also have a natural **instinct** to hunt and **explore**.

Overall, dogs are **intelligent**, social, and loyal animals that make great companions. Understanding their behavior and communication can help you develop a strong **bond** with your **furry** friend and ensure that they are happy and well-behaved members of society.

4. Language Practice

Complete the sentences using a word from the box.

- descended
- traits
- affection
- explore
- bond
- breeds
- thrive
- instinct
- intelligent
- furry

1) In a family, there's a strong (   ) between parents and children. They love and support each other through good times and bad.

2) At bedtime, I always sleep with my favorite (   ) teddy bear. It's so cuddly and makes me feel safe at night.

3) The fluffy snowflakes (   ) from the sky, covering the ground in a soft blanket of snow.

4) We're studying dinosaurs in class, and it's like going back in time to (   ) how they lived. It's fascinating to learn about creatures that roamed the Earth long ago.

5) Billy has been practicing his math skills every day, and he's starting to (   ) in class. His grades are improving, and he feels more confident.

6) At Thanksgiving, we express (   ) by sharing what we are thankful for. It's a time when families come together and show love.

7) Tom has a unique (   ) of hobbies. He enjoys both painting and playing the guitar, showing his artistic and musical sides.

8) We learned in class that animals have different (   ). Some birds can fly, while others have strong legs for running.

9) When we face a challenge, our (   ) is to keep trying and not give up. It's a natural feeling that helps us overcome difficulties.

10) Dolphins are known to be (   ) animals. They can do tricks and even communicate with each other using special sounds

5. Some General Facts about Dogs

- Dogs need regular exercise and mental stimulation to stay healthy and happy.

- Dogs have different temperaments and personalities, which can be influenced by breed, upbringing, and environment.

- Dogs have different socialization needs depending on their age, breed, and temperament.

- Dogs have basic needs such as food, water, shelter, exercise, and veterinary care.

- Dogs can exhibit a range of behaviors, such as jumping, digging, and chewing, which can be managed through training and appropriate outlets.

Here is an interesting story about dogs:

Hachiko, the loyal Akita: Hachiko was a Japanese Akita who lived in the 1920s. Every day, he would accompany his owner, a university professor, to the train station, and then wait for him to return from work. One day, the professor suffered a fatal stroke while at work and never returned to the train station. Despite this, Hachiko continued to wait at the station every day for nine years, hoping to see his owner again. Hachiko's loyalty touched the hearts of the Japanese people, and after his death, a statue was erected in his honor at the Shibuya train station in Tokyo.

출처: https://en.wikipedia.org/wiki/Akita_(dog)

6. Practical English

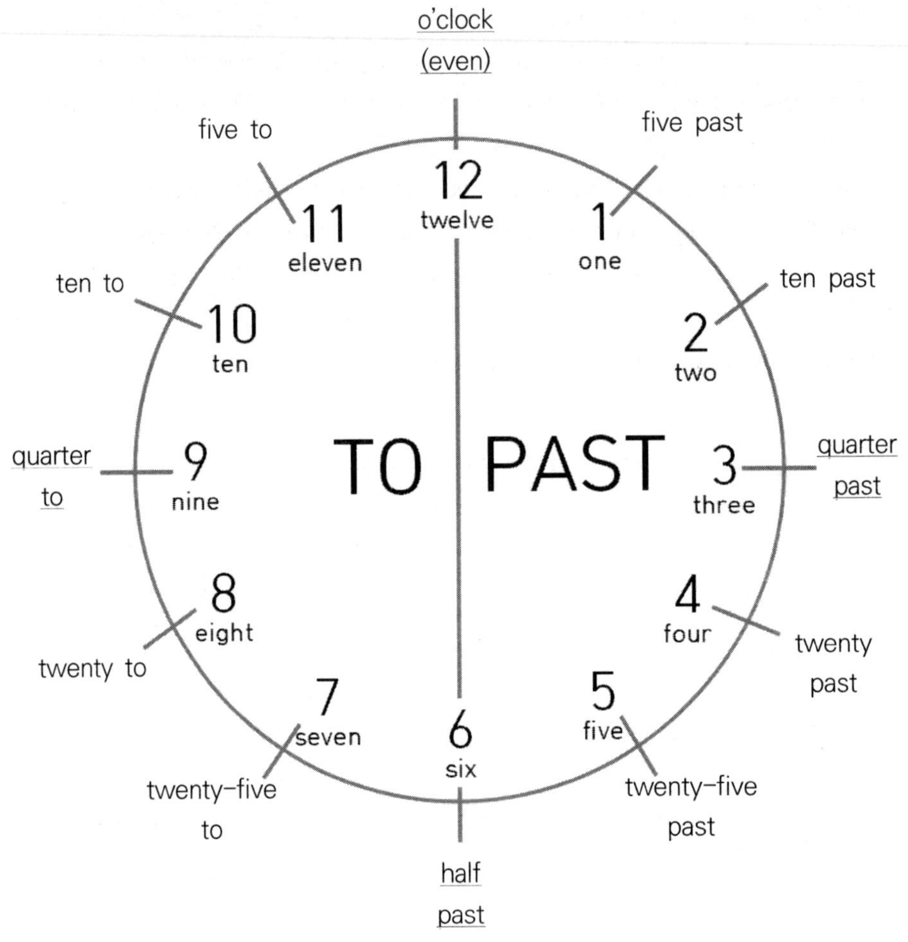

quarter : 1/4 (15분)
half : 절반 (30분)
hour - minute - second

[09:15]
It's nine fifteen.
It's a quarter past nine.
It's forty-five to ten.
It's nine quarter.
It's fifteen past nine.

Greetings in various situations I

Greetings can be expressed in various ways depending on the situation. Below are some common greeting expressions:

Normally Greeting:

Hello!

Hi there!

Hey!

A: Hello! How are you today?

B: Hi there! I'm doing well, thank you. How about you?

Morning/afternoon/evening greetings:

Good morning!

A: Good morning! Did you sleep well?

B: Good morning! Yes, I did. How about you?

Good afternoon!

Good evening!

A: Good afternoon! How's your day going so far?

B: Good evening! It's been a busy day, but not bad. How about yours?

Saying Hello:

How are you?

How's it going?

A: Hey, how are you doing these days?

B: I'm good, thanks for asking. How about yourself?

Self-introduction:

My name is [○○○].

I'm [○○○]. Nice to meet you.

A: Hi, I don't think we've met. I'm [A].

B: Nice to meet you, [A]. I'm [B].

Greetings from a close relationship:

What's up?

Howdy!

Long time no see!

A: What's up? Long time no see!

B: Hey! Yeah, it's been a while. How have you been?

Chapter 03

Dogs are wonderful animals

-About the attributes of dogs-

1. Word Preview

• ensure	• essential
• nutrition	• provide
• veterinarian	• vaccination
• injury	• appetite
• crucial	• obedient

• ensure

Please double-check your math homework to **ensure** you didn't make any mistakes.

① 책임지다, 보장[보증]하다, (성공 등을) 확실하게 하다; (지위 등을) 확보하다

• essential

For a successful camping trip, water and a tent are must-haves; they are **essential**.

① 근본적인, 필수의, 불가결한, 가장 중요한

• nutrition

Eating a variety of fruits and vegetables is part of healthy eating and good **nutrition**.

① 영양; 영양 공급 ② 자양물, 음식물

• **provide**

The teacher will **provide** us with the materials we need for the science experiment.

① 주다, 공급(지급)하다

• **veterinarian**

If your pet is sick, you should take them to the **veterinarian** to make them feel better.

① 수의사

• **vaccination**

Getting a **vaccination** is like putting on germ armor. It helps your body fight off germs and stay healthy.

① 백신 주사, 예방 접종

• **injury**

If you get a little **injury**, like a cut or a scrape, you can put a bandage on your ouchie or boo-boo.

① (사고 등에 의한) 상해, 부상 ② 손상, 손해

- **appetite**

My tummy is wanting food right now. I think I have a big **appetite** for dinner!" Feeling like eating

① 식욕 ② 욕구

- **crucial**

Bringing your homework back to school is very important. It's one of the most **crucial** things to remember.

① 결정적인, 중대한, 엄격한

- **obedient**

An **obedient** student is a good listener in class. They follow directions and pay attention to the teacher.

① 순종하는, 유순한, 고분고분한, 말 잘 듣는

2. Useful Expression

① Before you leave the classroom, **ensure** you have all your belongings." Double-check.

② Wearing a helmet is **essential** when riding a bike to ensure your safety.

③ Milk is good for your body because it provides important **nutrition** like calcium for strong bones.

④ During the school lunch, they offer a variety of **nutritious** foods to provide us with a balanced meal.

⑤ Our dog was not feeling well, so we took **veterinarian** to the pet vet for a check-up.

⑥ Think of a **vaccination** as a health booster shot. It helps your body become super strong and ready to fight off any sickness.

⑦ If you have a big **injury**, like falling off your bike, it might cause a hurt or owie, and you should tell an adult.

⑧ When I wake up in the morning, I have a feeling like eating breakfast because my **appetite** is ready for food.

⑨ Washing your hands before lunch is super necessary. It's a **crucial** step to keep everyone healthy.

⑩ Being **obedient** means following the rules at school. We should all be obedient to make our classroom a happy place.

3. Reading

If you are considering getting a dog or already have one, there are several things you need to know to **ensure** that you can provide a safe, healthy, and happy home for your furry friend. Some of the **essential** things you need to know include.

First of all, dogs need proper **nutrition**, exercise, and grooming to thrive. You should research the type of food your dog needs, how much to feed them, and how often. You should also **provide** your dog with regular exercise and keep them clean through regular grooming, such as bathing and brushing.

Regular visits to the **veterinarian** are essential to ensure your dog is healthy and up-to-date on **vaccinations**. You should also be aware of signs of illness or **injury**, such as vomiting, diarrhea, and changes in **appetite** or behavior.

And Proper training is **crucial** for dogs to become well-behaved and **obedient**. You should research different training methods and techniques to find what works best for you and your dog. Training can also help with bonding and socialization.

4. Language Practice

Complete the sentences using a word from the box.

Or match the words their meaning from the box.

• ensure	• essential
• nutrition	• provide
• veterinarian	• vaccinations
• injury	• appetite
• crucial	• obedient

1) This people are an important role of a dog's physical and mental health. Animal care specialist: (   )

2) When you're (   ), you do what you're told by your parents or teachers. It helps everything run smoothly.

3) Wearing a coat in the winter is really, really needed. It's (   ) to stay warm in the cold weather. "Super necessary".

4) When answering the question, be certain to read it carefully before writing your response. (   )

5) Eating fruits and vegetables is important for maintaining a healthy body. (   )

6) To stay strong and active, make sure you are eating the right foods that give your body the (   ) it needs.

7) Sometimes accidents happen, and you might get a little (   ). It's important to let someone know about your accident boo-boo so they can help.

8) Can you please give me a pencil? I forgot mine, and I need one for the test. (   ).

9) A (   ) is like a special shield that protects you from getting sick. It's your body's superhero power against germs.

10) When the pizza arrives, my friends and I are always ready to eat. Our (   ) for pizza is so big.

5. Some General Facts about Dogs
-Misunderstanding about dogs;

- One common misunderstanding related to dogs is the belief that all dogs are friendly and love to be petted. While many dogs are friendly and enjoy being around people, not all dogs have the same temperament.
  Some dogs may be fearful, anxious, or aggressive, especially if they have not been socialized properly or have had negative experiences in the past.

- Unfortunately, this misunderstanding can lead to dangerous situations where people approach unfamiliar dogs without caution, resulting in dog bites or attacks.
  It's important to remember that dogs, like people, have their own personalities and preferences, and it's important to approach them with respect and caution.
  Before approaching a dog, always ask the owner's permission and take cues from the dog's body language to determine if they are comfortable with interaction.

Here is an interesting story about dog:

Daisy, the cancer-sniffing dog: Daisy was a Labrador Retriever who was trained to detect cancer in humans. Her owner, Dr. Claire Guest, trained Daisy to detect the odor of cancer cells, and Daisy became very good at her job. She was able to detect cancer in urine samples with an accuracy rate of 93%, and she even detected cancer in her owner's breast six years before it was diagnosed by doctors. Daisy's incredible sense of smell helped to save countless lives and paved the way for further research into the use of dogs in medical detection.

출처: https://huffpost.com〉entry

6. Practical English

Greetings in various situations II

English greeting expressions available in business environments or at formal events:

Greetings from the office:

Good morning, [○○○]. How are you today?

Hello, everyone. I hope you're all doing well.

Meeting Start Greeting:

Ladies and gentlemen, good afternoon. Thank you for joining us today.

Good morning, team. Let's get started with today's agenda.

Let's begin our meeting. Good morning, everyone.

I'd like to call this meeting to order. Good afternoon, all.

✿ Greeting to the boss or the other party:

Mr./Ms. [○○○], it's a pleasure to meet you.

Hello [○○○], thank you for taking the time to meet with me.

Hi team, I trust you had a productive weekend.

Good evening, everyone. I'd like to acknowledge the hard work you've all put in.

✿ Greetings from Business Mail:

Dear [○○○],

I hope this email finds you well.

To whom it may concern,

I am writing to inform you about...

Meeting or event closing greetings:

Before we conclude, I'd like to thank each of you for your contributions today.

As we wrap up, I want to express my gratitude to everyone for their time and effort.

Expressing Appreciation:

Thank you for being here today.

I appreciate your attendance and participation.

수 읽기

기수	0 : Zero	서수
one	1	first
two	2	second
three	3	third
four	4	fourth
five	5	fifth
six	6	sixth
seven	7	seventh
eight	8	eighth
nine	9	ninth
ten	10	tenth
eleven	11	eleventh
twelve	12	twelfth

+ : plus	− : minus
× : times, multiple	÷ : devided by
. : point	= : equals
( ) : bracket	

분수(Fractions):

분자 (기수) 분모 (서수)	〈읽는 방법〉 ($4\frac{3}{5}$) ① 자연수(4) → 분자(3) → 분모(5) ② 분자가 2 이상이면 분모(서수)에 S가 붙습니다. ③ 자연수(4) and 분자(3)/기수 분모(5)/서수 +S = four and three fifths	〈Over〉 ($4\frac{3}{5}$) ① 자연수 and 분자 over 분모 ② 모두 기수 사용 = four and three over five

분자(위 숫자)는 기수로 분모(아래 숫자)는 서수 형태로 읽는다.

- 3/4 (three fourths)

$\frac{1}{5}$ (1/5) : one fifth	2/5 : two fifths
*주의	
1/2 : one second → one half = 50%(반)	2/3 : two thirds 분자가 2 이상 → third + s
1/4 : one fourth → one quarter = 1/4	3/4 : three fourths → three quarters 분자가 2 이상 → quarter에도 S 붙이기

〈읽어보기〉 $$4\frac{1}{3}\left(5+7\times\frac{1}{2}\right)=43.15$$

① (bracket → × → + → bracket)
② 밖에 있는 분수
③ = (equals)
① bracket seven times one half plus five bracket
② four and one third
③ equals forty three point one five

= bracket seven times one half plus five bracket four and one third equals forty three point one five

퍼센트(Percentages):

숫자를 읽은 후 “percent”를 추가한다.

25%: twenty-five percent

서수 (Ordinal Numbers):

12th: twelfth

각 자릿수의 가치에 해당하는 올바른 단위(ones, tens, hundreds, thousands, millions, billions 등)를 사용하고, 분수와 같은 특수 용어(“half”, “quarter”, “third” 등)

1/3: one-third

2/5: two-fifths

3/8: three-eighths

4/7: four-sevenths

5/6: five-sixths

소수 (Decimal Numbers):

소수점에 대해 "point"라고 읽는다.

소수점 뒤의 각 숫자를 개별적으로 읽는다.

3.14: three point one four

0.1: zero point one 또는 one-tenth.

0.25: zero point two-five 또는 twenty-five hundredths.

0.6: zero point six 또는 six-tenths.

1.2: one point two 또는 one and two-tenths.

2.75: two point seventy-five 또는 two and seventy-five hundredths.

0.25: zero point two-five 또는 twenty-five hundredths.

1.75: one point seventy-five 또는 one and seventy-five hundredths.

2.456: two point four five six 또는 two and four hundred fifty-six thousandths.

Chapter
04

About pet beauty Ⅰ

-A General understanding of pet beauty-

1. Word Preview

- aesthetic
- variety
- hygiene
- characteristics
- enhance
- appearance
- attractive
- approach
- sensitivity
- priority

• aesthetic

The fashion blogger has a keen eye for **aesthetics**, effortlessly combining colors and patterns in her outfits.

① 미학, 미적 미술의, 심미적인

• appearance

The actor's sudden change in **appearance** surprised everyone at the movie premiere.

① 출현 ② 기색, 징조; 현상 ③ 외관, 겉보기

• variety

The farmer grew a **variety** of crops in his fields, including corn, wheat, and soybeans.

① 변화, 다양(성) ② 가지각색의 것, 잡다한 것

- **attractive**

The colorful flowers in the garden added an **attractive** element to the overall landscape.

① 사람의 마음을 끄는; 매력적인, 애교 있는

- **hygiene**

Maintaining good **hygiene** is essential for preventing the spread of germs and maintaining overall health.

① 위생학(hygienics) ② 위생 상태; 위생

- **approach**

In order to solve the problem, we need to take a different **approach** and consider alternative solutions.

① 가까이 가다, ~에 접근하다

- **characteristics**

One **characteristic** of successful leaders is their ability to inspire and motivate others.

① 특질, 특색, 특징; 특성 ② 특성을 나타내도록

One characteristic of a successful entrepreneur is their ability to take calculated risks.

- **sensitivity**

The doctor showed great **sensitivity** in handling his client's emotional issues.

① 민감도, 자극 감응, 민감성

He approached the patient's emotional issues with care and sensitivity.

- **enhance**

Regular exercise can **enhance** your overall physical fitness and improve your health.

① 향상하다; (가치·능력·매력 따위를) 높이다, 늘리다, 더하다

Regular exercise can enhance both physical and mental well-being.

- **priority**

As a parent, ensuring the safety and well-being of my children is always my highest **priority**.

① 앞, 먼저임, 보다 중요함, 우선 ② 우선권, 선취권

2. Useful Expression

① I love the **aesthetic** of vintage clothing; the timeless style and unique details always catch my eye.

② Your **appearance**, like clean clothes and a friendly face, can help people feel comfortable around you.

③ The store offers a wide **variety** of products, catering to the diverse needs of its customers.

④ Your new haircut is so **attractive**! It really suits you and makes you look even more stylish

⑤ The restaurant received a low rating due to poor **hygiene** practices observed during a health inspection.

⑥ When faced with a difficult math problem, it's helpful to take a step-by-step **approach**. Break the problem down into smaller parts to make it easier to solve.

⑦ My dog has some unique **characteristics**. He's friendly, playful, and has a fluffy tail.

⑧ It's important to show **sensitivity** when someone is upset. Offer a listening ear and be understanding about their feelings.

⑨ Practicing regularly can **enhance** your soccer skills. Work on dribbling and shooting to become a better player.

⑩ When you have a lot of homework, it's important to set **priorities.**

3. Reading

What is beauty to animals? Isn't an animal a beauty in itself?

A general understanding of the beauty of pets is to improve their beauty more than it is now through the care, styling, and **aesthetic** consideration of the appearance of pets, mainly dogs and cats. It includes taking care of pets' physical **appearance**, making them look the best, and maintaining overall health.

It includes a **variety** of activities and techniques aimed at making pets look **attractive**, maintaining their **hygiene**, and promoting their overall well-being.

True pet beauty should always be **approached** with the comfort and well-being of pets in mind. Tools or actions for any beauty should be taken into account soft and safe technology, appropriate products, and personal needs, breed **characteristics**, and **sensitivity** of pets. It is also important to ensure that pets' natural behaviors and desires are not damaged for beauty.

While the beauty of a pet can be enjoyable and **enhance** the bond between the pet and its owner, it is important to note that its happiness and comfort should always be the top **priority**.

4. Language Practice

Complete the sentences using a word from the box.

Or match the words their meaning from the box.

• aesthetic	• appearance
• variety	• attractive
• hygiene	• approach
• characteristics	• sensitivity
• enhance	• priority

1) If you're shy, try taking a friendly (   ) when meeting new people.

2) My dog has some unique (   ). He's friendly, playful, and has a fluffy tail.

3) When meeting someone new, it's nice to smile and make a good first impression. (   )

4) Plants require (   ) to their needs. Make sure to water them regularly and provide the right amount of sunlight for optimal growth.

5) A pinch of salt can ( ) the flavor of your soup.

6) Start with the most challenging task as your top ( ) and work your way down the list.

7) I love the ( ) of vintage clothing; the timeless style and unique details always catch my eye.

8) I picked this dress as a gift because I thought the color and design would be ( ) to you. I hope you like it

9) Maintaining good personal ( ) is crucial for staying healthy. Remember to brush your teeth, wash your hands, and take regular showers

10) Including a ( ) of fruits and vegetables in your meals is essential for a balanced diet.

5. About pet beauty tools.

Brushes and Combs:

These are perhaps the most essential pet beauty tools. These are basic grooming tools used to remove loose fur, dirt, and debris from your pet's coat. There are many different types of brushes and combs available, including slicker brushes, pin brushes, and bristle brushes, each with their own unique features and benefits.

Different types of brushes and combs are available for different coat types, such as short-haired or long-haired, and different breeds. Some popular types of brushes include slicker brushes, pin brushes, and rubber brushes.

Here is an interesting story about dog:

Laika was a stray dog from Moscow, and in 1957, she became the first living creature to orbit the Earth. Laika was aboard the Soviet spacecraft Sputnik 2, paving the way for human space exploration. While her mission did not have a happy ending, as she perished in space, Laika's journey marked a significant milestone in space history, and her contribution to space exploration is remembered.

출처: www.reuters.com〉article

6. Practical English

Useful expressions for shopping I

Search for Goods(물품 찾기):

"Excuse me, where can I find men's shoes?"

"Can you point me to the [department] section?"

"I'm looking for [item]. Do you know where I can find it?"

Customer: Excuse me, where can I find the women's shoes?

Staff: Sure, the women's shoes are located in the shoe department, which is in the back of the store. Follow me, and I'll show you.

Price Inquiry(가격 문의):

"How much does this [item] cost?"

"What's the price of [product]?"

"Is there a discount on this [item]?"

Customer: How much does this jacket cost?

Staff: The jacket is $80. It's currently on sale, and you can get an additional 10% off.

Inquire about size and color(사이즈와 색상 문의):

"Do you have this in a different size?"

"Can I get this in another color?"

"What sizes do you have available for this [clothing item]?"

Customer: Do you have this dress in a size small?

Staff: Yes, we have it in small, medium, and large. Which color are you interested in.

Quality check(품질 확인):

"Can you tell me about the quality of this [product]?"

"Is this [item] durable?"

"What materials is this made of?"

Customer: Can you tell me about the quality of this blender?

Staff: This blender is known for its durability and performance. It's one of our best-sellers.

수 읽기

100	hundred
1,000	thousand
1,000,000	million
10억	billion
소	trillion

1,000 thousand 1천

ex) 3,250 = three thousand two hundred fifty

5,890 = five thousand eight hundred ninety

1,000,000 million 100만

ex) 8,256,001 = eight million two hundred fifty six thousand one

3,614,791 = three million six hundred fourteen thousand seven hundred ninety one

1,000,000,000 billion 10억

ex) 4,781,347,812 = four billion seven hundred eighty one million three hundred forty seven thousand eight hundred twelve

3,612,581,254 = three billion six hundred twelve million five hundred eighty one thousand two hundred fifty four

1,000,000,000,000 trillion 1조

Chapter 05

About pet beauty Ⅱ

-Describe your pet's beauty in five areas: Grooming and Nutrition

1. Word Preview

• grooming	• maintain
• trimming	• infection
• abnormality	• treatment
• nutrition	• contribute
• protein	• promote

• grooming

Taking time for personal **grooming** is essential. Comb your hair, brush your teeth, and make sure your clothes are clean for a neat appearance.

① 차림새를 단정하게 하기, 치장하기

• maintain

To **maintain** a clean home, make a schedule for household chores. Vacuum regularly, dust surfaces, and clean up after meals to keep your living space tidy.

① 지속(계속)하다, 유지하다

- **trimming**

I need to schedule a hair **trimming** appointment; my hair has gotten quite long.

① 정돈, 말끔하게 함, 다듬질 ② 깎아 다듬기, 손질.

- **infection**

I caught a cold last week, and now I'm dealing with a throat **infection** and congestion.

① 공기 전염, 병균 감염

- **abnormality**

The shape of this fruit is **abnormal**; it looks a bit different from the ones we usually see.

① 이상, 변칙, 비정상적인

- **treatment**

Using "helping medicine" introduces the idea of **treatment** as something that aids in the healing process.

① 취급; 대우 ② 처리(법)

- **nutrition**

This expression simplifies the concept of **nutrition** by associating it with foods that contribute to good health.

① 영양; 영양 공급 ② 자양물, 음식물 ③ 영양학.

- **contribute**

In our class, everyone's good behavior and hard work are like 'helping hands' that **contribute** to a happy learning environment.

① 기부하다, 기증하다 ② 기여하다

- **protein**

Eggs, meat, and beans are our 'grow-up foods' because they have a special ingredient called '**protein**' that helps us grow strong and healthy

① 단백질

- **promote**

Reading books every day can 'encourage learning' and **promote** our understanding of new and exciting things.

① 진전시키다, 장려하다 ② 승진시키다

2. Useful Expression

① Regular pet **grooming** is important for your dog's health. Brush their fur, trim their nails, and give them a bath to keep them clean and happy.

② It's important to communicate regularly to **maintain** a strong friendship. Check in on your friends, listen to their concerns, and share your experiences to stay connected.

③ The function includes a text **trimming** feature to remove any unnecessary white spaces at the beginning and end of a string.

④ It's important to keep the wound clean and properly bandaged to avoid any bacterial **infections**.

⑤ Using "**abnormality**" is a simpler way to convey the idea of something being different from what is expected.

⑥ This expression simplifies the concept of **treatment** by associating it with something that helps make you feel better.

⑦ This expression connects **nutrition** with the idea of growing up and emphasizes the importance of certain foods for healthy development.

⑧ Everyone's positive actions **contribute** to a positive classroom atmosphere.

⑨ Nuts and cheese are like 'powerful foods' because they have **protein**, and eating them gives us the energy to play and learn.

⑩ Eating fruits and vegetables every day can '**promote** healthy habits' and help us grow strong and stay fit.

3. Reading

-Describe your pet's beauty in five areas: **Grooming and Nutrition**

Grooming:

Regular grooming is essential to **maintain** a pet's appearance. This includes brushing their fur, **trimming** their nails, and cleaning their ears and teeth.

Grooming is not just about making a pet look good. It is also essential for maintaining their overall health and well-being. Regular grooming can help prevent skin **infections**, matting, and other issues. It can also help pet owners detect lumps, bumps, or other skin **abnormalities** early, which can lead to timely **treatment** and better outcomes.

Nutrition:

Feeding pets a balanced and nutritious diet can **contribute** to their overall health and appearance. A healthy diet can result in a shiny coat, bright eyes, and a healthy weight.

A balanced and nutritious diet is essential for a pet's health and appearance. Poor nutrition can lead to a dull coat, dry skin, and other skin problems. A diet that is rich in **protein**, healthy fats, and vitamins can help **promote** a shiny coat, healthy skin, and strong nails.

4. Language Practice

Complete the sentences using a word from the box.

Or match the words their meaning from the box.

• grooming	• maintain
• trimming	• infections
• abnormalities	• treatment
• nutrition	• contributing
• protein	• promote

1) Exercise and a balanced diet are crucial to (   ) good physical health.

2) In this example, "(   )" refers to cutting or reducing the length of hair. It's a common term used in the context of haircare and grooming.

3) Before a job interview, pay attention to (   ). Dress appropriately, ensure your hair is tidy, and maintain good overall hygiene to make a positive impression.

4) Being kind and sharing toys can 'build friendship' and ( ) a happy and supportive classroom environment.

5) This expression uses the term "powerful foods" to convey the idea that ( )-rich foods provide energy for various activities.

6) Out of the Ordinary: Today's weather is out of the ordinary. It's not what we usually experience during this season. ( )

7) Make sure to regularly update your antivirus software to protect your computer from potential ( ).

8) Milk and cheese are our 'grow-up foods' because they help our bones grow strong and make us tall and healthy. ( )

9) If you have a boo-boo, you might put on a bandage and use a 'helping medicine' to make it feel better. ( )

10) This expression combines teamwork with the idea of ( ) individual efforts to create a collective achievement.

5. About pet beauty tools.

Clippers and Trimmers:

Clippers and trimmers are used to cut or trim your pet's fur. They come in different sizes and can be used to trim everything from your pet's face and ears to their entire body. Some clippers are cordless for added convenience, while others are designed to be used with a cord for more power.

Clippers and trimmers are used to give pets a haircut or trim their fur. They come in different sizes and types, including electric and manual, and are designed to cater to different coat types and lengths. They are particularly useful for pets with thick fur, such as dogs or cats.

Here is an interesting story about dog:

Rin Tin Tin was a German Shepherd rescued from a World War I battlefield by American soldier Lee Duncan. He went on to become a major Hollywood star in the 1920s and 1930s, appearing in numerous films and TV shows. Rin Tin Tin's intelligence and charisma made him one of the most famous and beloved dogs in the entertainment industry, and his legacy continues to influence canine actors today.

출처: https://en.wikipedia.org/wiki/Rin_Tin_Tin

6. Practical English

Useful expressions for shopping II

Discounts and benefits(할인과 혜택):

"Are there any discounts or promotions today?"

"Do you offer any student/military/senior discounts?"

"Is there a loyalty program I can sign up for?"

Customer: Are there any discounts or promotions today?

Staff: Yes, we have a promotion on electronics today. You can save 15% on all electronics purchases.

✿ Payment and calculation(결제와 계산):

"Can I pay with a credit card/cash?"

"Is there an additional charge for using a credit card?"

"Could I get a receipt, please?"

Customer: Can I pay with a credit card?

Staff: Certainly. We accept all major credit cards. Would you like to pay here at the counter?

✿ Exchange and Refund(교환 및 환불):

"What is your return/exchange policy?"

"Can I get a refund if I change my mind?"

"How long do I have to return this [item]?"

Customer: What is your return policy?

Staff: We offer a 30-day return policy with a receipt. If you change your mind or encounter any issues, feel free to bring it back.

when you need help(도움이 필요한 경우):

"Could you help me with something, please?"

"Do you have a shopping assistant available?"

"I'm having trouble finding [item]. Can you assist me?"

Customer: Could you help me find a gift for my friend?

Staff: Of course! What are your friend's interests, and do you have a specific budget in mind? I can suggest some options.

What's the most used English expression on the phone

전화 Telephone	전화 걸고 받기 Making & Answering a Call
• cellular phone • answering machine • unlisted number • directory assistance • extension (number) • direct line • local code • national number • local call • long-distance call • international call • collect call	• call someone : ~에게 전화하다 = make a call to someone • put A through to B : A의 전화를 B에게 연결해주다 (connect/transfer) • receive a call : 전화를 받다 • pick up the phone : 수화기를 들다 • put someone on hold : ~을 기다리게 하다 • speak to[with] someone : ~와 전화하다 • wait for a dial phone : 통화음이 울리길 기다리다 • hang up the phone : 전화를 끊다 • dial : 다이얼을 돌리다 전화를 걸다 • redial: 전화를 다시 걸다 • hold on : (전화를 끊지 않고) 잠시 기다리다

This is she / This is he / speaking	저예요
hold on, please / put on hold, please / Don't hang up the phone	잠시만 기다려주세요

Chapter 06

About pet beauty Ⅲ

-Describe your pet's beauty in five areas: Exercise, Breeding

1. Word Preview

• weight	• prevent
• obesity	• boredom
• diabete	• breed
• distinctive	• adopt
• shelter	• benefit

• weight

Compare the backpack and the pencil. The backpack is heavy, and the pencil is light. We use ‘heavy’ and ‘light’ to talk about **weight**.

① 무게, 중량, 체중; 비만

• prevent

Washing our hands before eating helps ‘fight germs’ and **prevent** us from getting sick.

① 막다, 방해하다, 막아서 …못 하게 하다

- **obesity**

his expression encourages physical activity without directly addressing the concept of **obesity.**

① 비만, 비대

- **boredom**

Turn '**boredom**' into creativity time! Grab some paper and colors, and see what amazing drawings or crafts you can create.

① 권태, 지루함

- **diabete**

This expression encourages children to make nutritious food choices without directly addressing the concept of **diabetes**.

① 당뇨병

- **breed**

There are many 'different types of pets' or 'animal **breeds**' like dogs and cats. Each one is special and unique!

① (새끼를) 낳다 ② 기르다; 양육하다, 가르치다

- **distinctive**

Each person in our class is '**distinctive**.' We all have different talents and qualities that make us stand out.

① 독특한, 특이한, 구별이 분명한

- **adopt**

When you 'make someone part of the family', it means you **adopt** them.

① 양자로 삼다 ② (의견·방침·조처 따위를) 채용, 채택하다

- **shelter**

An animal **shelter** is a 'home for animals' that don't have families.

① 피난 장소, 은신처, 대합실, 대피호

- **benefit**

Eating fruits and vegetables has a '**benefit**' because it helps our bodies grow strong and healthy.

① 이익, 이득 ② 은혜

2. Useful Expression

① Let's use a balance scale to see which toy is heavier. The side that goes down is the 'heavier' one because it has more **weight**.

② This expression uses "germ fighters" to convey the idea that handwashing can **prevent** illness by keeping germs away.

③ "Eating lots of colorful fruits and vegetables helps our bodies grow strong. Let's 'eat colorful foods' every day!" This expression emphasizes the importance of a balanced diet without using the term "**obesity**"

④ If you ever feel '**bored**,' try exploring new games or activities. There are so many fun things to discover!

⑤ Running, jumping, and playing games emphasize the importance of physical activity for overall health without specifically mentioning **diabetes**.

⑥ In our school garden, we grow a 'variety of plants' or 'plant **breeds**,' like roses and sunflowers. They come in different shapes and colors!

⑦ This **distinctive** expression focuses on the idea that everyone is special and has unique qualities.

⑧ We decided to 'bring home a friend' from the animal shelter and **adopt** a cute kitten. Now, we have a new furry family member!

⑨ People visit **shelters** to adopt pets and give them a loving home.

⑩ Reading books every day is a '**benefit**' because it's fun and helps our imagination grow.

3. Reading

-Describe your pet's beauty in five areas: **Exercise, Breeding**

- **Exercise:**

Exercise helps pets maintain a healthy **weight**, which can enhance their appearance. Regular exercise can also help to **prevent** health issues such as **obesity** and joint problems.

Exercise is essential for pets to maintain a healthy weight and stay active. Exercise can also help reduce stress, prevent **boredom**, and promote good sleep, which can lead to a better overall appearance. Regular exercise can also help prevent some common health problems such as obesity, **diabetes**, and joint problems.

- **Breeding:**

Certain **breeds** of pets are known for their beauty and **distinctive** features. However, it is important to note that breeding for certain physical traits can lead to health problems.

Adopting a pet from a **shelter** can be a great option for those who are primarily concerned with a pet's health and personality rather than its appearance. You could discuss the **benefits** of adopting pets from shelters.

4. Language Practice

Complete the sentences using a word from the box.

Or match the words their meaning from the box.

- weight
- obesity
- diabete
- distinctive
- shelter
- prevent
- boredom
- breed
- adopt
- benefit

1) Here, the expression highlights the enjoyment and mental growth as of (   ) reading.

2) A (   ) is like a 'safe place for friends'. Sometimes people don't have homes, and shelters help them stay safe and find a place to sleep.

3) Crayons come in many colors, and each color is like a different crayon (   ). Let's use them to create colorful drawings!

4) Eating fruits and vegetables is good for us because they have the right '(　　　　　)' of vitamins and minerals to keep our bodies strong.

5) "Eating lots of colorful fruits and vegetables helps our bodies grow strong. Let's 'eat colorful foods' every day!" This expression emphasizes the importance of a balanced diet without using the term "(　　　　　)."

6) Wearing helmets and knee pads when riding bikes can 'keep us safe' and (　　　　　) injuries.

7) The artwork you create is 'one-of-a-kind'. No one else can make the same picture because it's uniquely yours. This expression emphasizes the uniqueness and individuality of something. (　　　　　)

8) Encouraging children to read is a great way to combat (　　　　　) by engaging their imagination in exciting stories.

9) Drinking water instead of sugary drinks is a 'healthy habit' that makes us feel good and keeps our bodies happy. This expression focuses on promoting the habit of choosing water over sugary beverages for good health without using the term (　　　　　).

10) Just like how families can (　　　　) pets or even children who need a loving home.

5. The Importance of Grooming for Pet Beauty

The Importance of Grooming for Pet Beauty:

1. Keeps the Coat Shiny and Healthy: Regular brushing and bathing help to remove dirt and dead skin cells from a pet's coat, making it look shiny and healthy.

2. Prevents Tangles and Mats: Grooming helps to prevent tangles and mats in a pet's fur, which can be painful and uncomfortable.

3. Reduces Shedding: Regular grooming can help to reduce shedding, which is a common problem for many pets.

4. Controls Fleas and Ticks: Grooming helps to control flea and tick infestations by removing these pests from a pet's coat.

5. Promotes Bonding: Grooming provides an opportunity for owners to bond with their pets and show them affection.

► **Cue discrimination**

In dog training, "cue discrimination" refers to the process of teaching a dog to differentiate and respond appropriately to different cues or signals. It involves training a dog to recognize and understand specific cues or commands and to respond differently based on the cue given.

Here is an interesting story about dog:

Smoky, a Yorkshire Terrier, became a war hero during World War II. She was found by an American soldier in an abandoned foxhole in the Pacific. Smoky went on to accompany her owner, Corporal William A. Wynne, throughout the war, participating in over 150 air raids and surviving 12 combat missions. Smoky's small size allowed her to complete tasks in tight spaces that humans couldn't, and she became a morale booster for troops. After the war, Smoky continued to bring joy to hospitals and veterans' homes.

출처: https://en.wikipedia.org/wiki/Smoky_(dog)

6. Practical English

useful expressions in banking I

Opening an Account(계좌 개설):

“I'd like to open a checking/savings account, please.”

”What documents do I need to open an account?”

“Can you explain the different types of accounts you offer?”

Deposits and Withdrawals(입출금):

“I'd like to make a deposit into my account.”

“Could you please help me withdraw some cash?”

“Is there a fee for withdrawing money from an ATM?”

Checking an Account Balance(계좌 잔액 확인):

"Could you check my account balance, please?"

"What's the current balance in my account?"

"Is there a way to check my balance online?"

Transfers(송금):

"I need to transfer money to another account."

"What information do I need for a bank transfer?"

"How long does it take for a transfer to be completed?"

Loans(대출):

"I'm interested in applying for a personal/home/auto loan."

"What are the interest rates for loans currently?"

"What documents are required for a loan application?"

Chapter
07

About pet beauty Ⅳ
–Describe your pet's beauty in five areas: Personality

1. Word Preview

- overall
- socialize
- expose
- confident
- command
- discuss
- behavior
- situation
- outgoing
- lead

• overall

I did well on my homework **overall**, but I struggled with one question.

① 전체적, 종합적으로 보면

• discuss

Today I **discussed** the characteristics of democracy and socialism with my students.

① 토론, 논의하다

• socialize

I love to **socialize** with my coworkers during lunch breaks, as it helps build a stronger team bond.

① 사회적[사교적]으로 하다, 사회화하다

- **behavior**

he teacher commended Sarah for her exemplary **behavior** in class, noting her attentiveness and respectful interactions with classmates.

① 행동, 행실; 동작, 태도, 품행

- **expose**

During our science class, we will **expose** different objects to sunlight to see how they react to the heat.

① (햇볕·바람·비 따위에) 쐬다, 맞히다, 노출시키다

- **situation**

In the story we read, the main characters faced a tricky **situation** when they got lost in the enchanted forest.

① 위치, 장소, 소재, 환경② 입장, 사정

- **confident**

Kelly felt **confident** when she gave her presentation to the class, and everyone applauded for her hard work.

① 확신하는 ② 자신이 있는, 자신만만한

- **outgoing**

Jay is very **outgoing** and always makes new friends easily because she loves talking to people.

① 나가는, 출발하는, 은퇴하는 ② 사교적, 개방적인

- **command**

The teacher gave a **command** for the students to line up quietly and follow her to the cafeteria for lunch.

① 에게 명(령)하다, …에게 호령하다, 요구하다 ② 지휘하다, …의 지휘권을 갖다; 통솔하다

- **lead**

Mike was chosen to lead the class project because he is organized and great at working with others.

① 이끌다, 인도, 안내하다, 데리고 가다 ② …이 손을 잡아 이끌다

2. Useful Expression

① The **overall** mood in the classroom was cheerful as the students prepared for the upcoming school assembly.

② Today I **discussed** the characteristics of democracy and socialism with my students.

③ It's important for teenagers to **socialize** with their peers to develop social skills and form meaningful connections.

④ Parents play a crucial role in shaping their children's **behavior** by providing positive reinforcement and setting clear expectations.

⑤ The teacher will **expose** us to new and exciting books in the library to encourage a love for reading.

⑥ During our class discussion, the teacher asked us how we would handle a **situation** where a friend needed help with their homework.

⑦ Even though it was his first soccer game, Timmy played with **confidence** and scored a goal for his team.

⑧ During group projects, the teacher appreciates **outgoing** students who share their ideas and work well with their classmates.

⑨ During the game, the coach will give a **command** for the players to pass the ball to their teammates to score points.

⑩ In the school play, Jake was excited to **lead** the group of actors as the main character in the story.

3. Reading

Describe your pet's beauty in five areas: **Personality**

- **Personality:**

A pet's personality can also contribute to their **overall** beauty. A pet's personality can be just as important as its appearance. You could **discuss** the importance of training and **socializing** pets to help them develop good **behavior**. A happy and well-behaved pet can be a joy to be around and can enhance their owner's life.

Socialization **exposes** pets to a variety of people, animals, and **situations** from an early age helps them adapt well and become **confident**. This can lead to a happier, more **outgoing** pet that is a pleasure to be around.

Training pets to follow basic **commands** and rules can help them become better-behaved and more obedient. This can **lead** to a stronger bond between pet and owner

4. Language Practice

Complete the sentences using a word from the box.

Or match the words their meaning from the box.

• overall	• discuss
• socialize	• behavior
• expose	• situation
• confident	• outgoing
• command	• lead

1) When playing on the playground, it's important to know what to do in a (   ) where someone gets hurt, like informing a teacher or finding a playground supervisor.

2) During the field trip, the teacher asked a responsible student to (   ) the line as they walked through the museum.

3) Even introverts can find enjoyable ways to (   ), such as attending small gatherings or joining online communities with shared interests

4) I did well on my homework (   ), but I struggled with one question.

5) In a professional setting, it's essential to maintain professional (   ), treating colleagues with respect and conducting oneself in a manner that reflects well on the company.

6) At recess, the (   ) kids organize games and invite others to join, making sure everyone has a chance to play and have fun.

7) In art class, we will learn about various painting techniques and be (   ) to different styles of art.

8) After practicing their spelling words every day, the students felt (   ) about the upcoming spelling bee.

9) We (   ) the roles of each group's assignment.

10) In computer class, the teacher showed us how to use a keyboard and gave us a (   ) to press the 'Enter' key after typing our names.

5. Some General Facts about Dogs

Exercise and Pet Beauty

Regular exercise is an important aspect of pet care that can contribute to a pet's overall beauty. Here are some ways that exercise affects pet beauty:

1. Healthy Weight: Regular exercise can help pets maintain a healthy weight, which can enhance their appearance and prevent health problems.

2. Strong Muscles: Exercise can help build and maintain strong muscles, which can contribute to a pet's overall appearance.

3. Good Posture: Regular exercise can help pets maintain good posture, which can enhance their appearance and prevent health problems.

4. Mental Health: Regular exercise can help to reduce stress and anxiety, which can contribute to a pet's overall well-being and beauty.

Here is an interesting story about dog:

In 1925, the town of Nome, Alaska, faced a diphtheria outbreak, and the only way to deliver the life-saving antitoxin serum was by dog sled. Balto, a Siberian Husky, led his team through treacherous conditions during the "Great Race of Mercy." Balto and his musher, Gunnar Kaasen, covered the longest and most dangerous leg of the journey, ultimately delivering the serum to Nome and preventing a widespread epidemic. Balto's heroics made him a national hero, and a statue in his honor stands in New York City's Central Park.

출처: https://en.wikipedia.org/wiki/Siberian_Husky

6. Practical English

useful expressions in banking II

Credit/Debit Cards:

I need to activate my new credit/debit card.

What's my credit card limit?

Transfers and Fees(이체와 수수료):

Are there any fees for transferring money between my accounts?

Can you explain the fees associated with this service?

Statements(이력서 관련):

Can I receive my bank statements electronically?

When are the monthly statements usually generated?

Security(보안):

What security measures are in place to protect my account?

Can I set up two-factor authentication for my online banking?

Deposit(예금)

During our class fundraiser, students were asked to make a deposit of at least a dollar into the collection box to support the charity."

Sally's dad explained to her that when he goes to the bank, he makes a deposit by putting money into his account to save for family activities.

Withdrawal(인출)

Yesterday, Johnny made a withdrawal from his piggy bank to buy a new video game he had been saving up for.

Samantha's mom explained that when she goes to the bank, she makes a money withdrawal to get cash for groceries and other family expenses.

Transfer(이체)

Mom needed to send money to Grandma for her birthday, so she used a money transfer service to make sure it reached her quickly.

As part of our math lesson, the teacher explained how a money transfer works when you want to give some of your allowance to a friend using a secure method.

Loan(대출)

Jack's parents took out a loan to help buy a new car, and they explained to him that it's like borrowing money and paying it back over time.

“The teacher told the class about a special program that provides students with a loan for books, allowing them to borrow textbooks for the school year.

Interest(이자)

During show-and-tell, Emily shared her collection of seashells, capturing the interest of her classmates with the different shapes and colors.

The teacher encouraged students to choose books that sparked their interest during library time, so they could enjoy reading about topics they found exciting.

✿ Account Balance(계좌 잔고)

During math class, the teacher taught us about keeping track of our account balance in a pretend bank account as part of a budgeting lesson.

As a class treasurer, Tim had to update the class account balance regularly, ensuring we had enough funds for upcoming school activities.

✿ Transfer Fee(이체 수수료)

When Sally wanted to switch schools, her parents had to pay a transfer fee to cover the costs of processing her enrollment in the new school.

During our math lesson, Mr. Johnson explained the concept of a transfer fee as the extra money you might need to pay when moving funds from one account to another.

Statement(계좌 명세서)

As part of our science project, we had to write a statement about our hypothesis and what we learned from our experiments.

The librarian gave us a statement after we returned our library books, showing the titles we borrowed and the date they were due.

ATM(Automated Teller Machine)

Mom took me to the ATM to get some cash for our weekend trip, and I saw how the machine gives you money when you put in a card.

In our community project, we raised money for the animal shelter, and people could donate by putting cash in the donation box or using the ATM at the local bank.

Chapter
08

Dog Training Ⅰ

1. Word Preview

- patience
- reinforcement
- boundary
- Ignore
- harmful
- consistency
- establish
- reward
- punish
- counterproductive

• patience

While waiting in line for the school bus, the teacher reminded the students to practice **patience** and take turns getting on.

① 인내(력), 참을성; 끈기

• consistency

The teacher emphasized the importance of **consistency** in completing homework assignments, reminding the students to turn in their work on time every day.

① 일관성; 언행일치 ② 조화 ③ 농도, 밀도

- **reinforcement**

The teacher used positive **reinforcement** by giving stickers to students who completed their assignments on time, encouraging them to continue working hard.

① 강화 요법

- **establish**

In the beginning of the school year, the teacher worked hard to **establish** a positive and welcoming classroom environment for all the students.

① 설립하다, 창립하다, 수립하다, 확립하다

- **boundary**

The teacher explained the playground **boundaries** to the students, reminding them to play within the designated areas for safety.

① 경계(선), 한계, 범위, 영역

- **reward**

John received a reward for finishing his homework early – a special sticker from the teacher.

① 보수, 포상, 현상금, 사례금 ② 보답, 응보

- **Ignore**

During the game, Timmy chose to **ignore** his friend's teasing and continued playing with a smile on his face.

① 무시하다, 묵살하다, 모른 체하다 ② 기각하다.

- **punish**

When students misbehave in class, the teacher might choose to **punish** them with a timeout or loss of a privilege.

① 사람 또는 죄를 벌하다, 응징하다

- **harmful**

The teacher reminded the students that name-calling and teasing can be **harmful** and hurtful to others, promoting a culture of kindness instead

① 해로운, 해가 되는

- **counterproductive**

Talking loudly during class is **counterproductive** because it disrupts the learning environment for everyone.

① 의도와는 반대된, 역효과의

2. Useful Expression

① During art class, Tom showed great **patience** as he carefully painted each detail on his project, creating a beautiful masterpiece.

② Kelly's **consistent** effort in practicing the piano paid off when she performed confidently during the school talent show.

③ During the spelling bee, the students received **reinforcement** from their classmates, who cheered them on as they spelled difficult words.

④ During the science experiment, we needed to **establish** a fair test by keeping all variables constant except for the one we were testing.

⑤ During group activities, it's important to respect each other's ideas and establish **boundaries** to make sure everyone feels comfortable participating.

⑥ During the spelling bee, the students were excited about the prospect of a **reward** for those who spelled all the words correctly.

⑦ The teacher encouraged the students to **ignore** distractions and focus on their work during the quiet reading time.

⑧ The school has a clear set of rules, and if someone breaks them, there may be consequences to help them learn from their mistakes rather than simply to **punish**.

⑨ During science class, we learned about the **harmful** effects of littering on the environment and why it's essential to keep our surroundings clean.

⑩ Skipping the steps in a math problem is **counterproductive**, as it can lead to mistakes in finding the correct solution.

3. Reading

Training a pet dog requires **patience**, **consistency**, and **positive reinforcement**. Here are some steps to train your pet dog:

Establish Rules and Boundaries:

Start by establishing rules and boundaries for your dog. Decide on what is and isn't acceptable behavior, and be consistent in enforcing those rules.

Use Positive Reinforcement:

Positive reinforcement is the best way to train your dog. **Reward** good behavior with treats, praise, and attention. **Ignore** or redirect bad behavior without **punishing** the dog.

Dogs respond well to positive reinforcement, so be sure to reward your dog with treats, praise, or playtime when they follow your commands. Avoid punishing your dog or using physical force as this can be **harmful** and **counterproductive**.

Start with Basic Commands:

Start with basic commands like "sit", "stay", "come", and "heel". Use positive reinforcement to encourage the dog to follow these commands.

Be Consistent:

Consistency is key when training a dog. Use the same commands and rewards every time, and make sure everyone in the household is using the same commands and rewards.

4. Language Practice

Complete the sentences using a word from the box.

Or match the words their meaning from the box.

• patience	• consistency
• reinforcement	• establish
• boundary	• reward
• Ignore	• punish
• harmful	• counterproductive

1) The librarian asked the students to be mindful of the quiet reading area (   ), ensuring that everyone can enjoy a peaceful reading environment.

2) In the story we read, the character learned that it's better to talk and find solutions than to (   ) others for misunderstandings.

3) During the science experiment, the students were instructed to observe and record data with (   ) to ensure accurate results.

4) The teacher promised a (   ) to the class if they worked together to complete a challenging project, motivating everyone to contribute their best efforts.

5) The teacher explained that arguing over small issues is (   ) to building a positive and supportive classroom community.

6) In the playground, the teacher praised the students for demonstrating (   ) while waiting for their turn on the swings and slides.

7) The principal praised the students for their good behavior at the assembly, providing (   ) for following the school's expectations.

8) Kelly decided to (   ) the negative comments and instead surrounded herself with friends who appreciated and supported her.

9) The school decided to (   ) a new reading program to encourage students to develop a love for books and improve their literacy skills.

10) The school counselor explained to the students that spreading rumors can be (   ) and can lead to misunderstandings, encouraging them to think before they speak.

5. Dog training terminology

Remember that training your dog takes time, patience, and dedication. With consistent effort and positive reinforcement, you can teach your pet good behavior and build a strong bond with your furry companion.

Sit:

A command used to ask the dog to sit down on its haunches.

This is one of the basic commands that trainers teach dogs. The dog is asked to sit down and stay in that position until given another command.

Stay:

A command used to ask the dog to remain in one place until further instructions are given.

This command is used to train dogs to remain in one position for a period of time. The dog is asked to sit, lie down or stand, and then stay in that position until given another command.

Come:

A command used to ask the dog to come towards the trainer.

This command is used to get the dog to come to the trainer. It is often used when the dog is off-leash and needs to be brought back to the trainer.

Heel:

A command used to ask the dog to walk closely beside the trainer's leg.

This command is used to train the dog to walk alongside the trainer in a controlled manner. The dog is expected to stay close to the trainer's leg and not pull on the leash.

Down:

A command used to ask the dog to lie down on the ground.

This command is used to train the dog to lie down on command. The dog is expected to stay in that position until given another command.

Off:

A command used to ask the dog to get off something, such as furniture or people.

This command is used to train the dog to get off furniture or stop jumping up on people. It is used to discourage unwanted behavior.

Here is an interesting story about dog:

> Chips was a German Shepherd–Collie–Husky mix that served in the U.S. Army during World War II. Trained as a sentry dog, Chips participated in the invasion of Sicily in 1943. During an attack on an enemy machine-gun nest, Chips broke free from his handler and attacked the enemy soldiers, forcing them to surrender. Chips' bravery earned him a Purple Heart and the Silver Star, making him the most decorated war dog of World War II. Despite initially being awarded these honors, they were later revoked due to military policy at the time, but Chips remains a symbol of courage and loyalty.

출처: https://en.wikipedia.org/wiki/Chips_(dog)

6. Practical English

Useful expressions for Tourism I

Airport:

Customer: Excuse me, where is the check-in counter?

Staff: The check-in counter is straight ahead, near the entrance.

Customer: Thank you. And where is the security checkpoint?

Staff: After check-in, follow the signs to security. It's on your right.

Hotel:

Customer: Hi, I have a reservation under [your name].

Receptionist: Welcome! Can I see your ID, please?

Customer: Sure, here it is. What time is check-in and check-out?

Receptionist: Check-in is at 3 PM, and check-out is at 11 AM.

Dining(음식 주문):

Customer: Could I see the menu, please?

Waiter: Of course. Here you go. Are you ready to order?

Customer: I'm allergic to nuts. Is there any dish without nuts?

Waiter: Absolutely, I can recommend a nut-free option.

Sightseeing(관광지):

Customer: How do I get to the museum from here?

Local: It's about a 10-minute walk. Just follow this street.

Customer: What time does the museum open and close?

Local: It opens at 9 AM and closes at 6 PM.

Checking the Schedule(일정 확인):

Customer: What time is the next train/bus to [destination]?

Station Staff: The next train to [destination] is at 2:30 PM from platform 3.

Chapter
09

Dog Training Ⅱ

1. Word Preview

• frequent	• aim
• gradually	• duration
• comfortable	• environment
• manage	• tempt
• experience	• interactive

• frequent

The teacher encourages **frequent** practice of spelling words to help students improve their language skills.

① 자주 일어나는, 빈번한, 횟수를 거듭하는, 여러 번의

• aim

In our math class, our **aim** is to learn multiplication tables up to 10 by the end of the semester.

① 겨냥하다, 겨누어 을 던지다

- **gradually**

Tom found learning to tie his shoes challenging at first, but **gradually**, with practice, he became really good at it.

① 차차로, 서서히

- **duration**

The teacher explained that the **duration** of the math test would be 45 minutes, and then we could move on to the next subject.

① 내구, 지속, 계속기간

- **comfortable**

The teacher rearranged the classroom seating so everyone could feel **comfortable** and focus on their lessons.

① 기분 좋은, 편한, 위안의; 고통이 없는

- **environment**

Our school works hard to create a positive learning **environment** where everyone feels welcome and included.

① 주위를 에워싸는 것, 환경

- **manage**

The teacher taught us how to **manage** our time by creating a daily schedule for homework, play, and chores.

① (사람·말·도구 따위를) 잘 다루다, 마음대로 움직이다; (기계·배 따위를) 조종하다

- **tempt**

Even though the cookies were for a bake sale, the delicious smell **tempted** the students not to wait until it was over to have a taste.

① 의 마음을 끌다, 유혹하다, 부추기다 ② 할 기분이 나게 하다, 꾀다

- **experience**

During our nature walk, the students had the opportunity to **experience** the sights and sounds of the forest, observing plants and animals.

① 경험, 체험, 견문; 경력; 경험

- **interactive**

The computer game was designed to be **interactive**, encouraging players to answer questions and solve puzzles to advance to the next level.

① 상호 작용하는, 서로 영향을 미치는

2. Useful Expression

① We have **frequent** fire drills at school to make sure we know what to do in case of an emergency.

② As part of our physical education class, we practice throwing a ball at a target to improve our **aim** and coordination.

③ Mrs. Johnson introduced new vocabulary words to the class **gradually**, making sure everyone had time to understand and use them in sentences.

④ During the school assembly, the principal announced that the **duration** of the upcoming play would be about 30 minutes, so everyone could plan accordingly.

⑤ The school nurse provided a **comfortable** space in the clinic for students who weren't feeling well, offering a quiet place to rest.

⑥ The teacher set up a quiet reading **environment** with soft lighting and comfortable cushions for the students to enjoy their books.

⑦ Tim learned how to **manage** his frustration by taking deep breaths and asking for help when he was struggling with his math homework

⑧ During the science experiment, the bubbling chemicals might **tempt** you to touch, but it's important to follow safety rules.

⑨ In music class, the teacher introduced different instruments, allowing the students to **experience** the joy of playing and creating music.

⑩ During science class, the students had an **interactive** experiment, mixing colors and observing the exciting reactions

3. Reading

Practice Every Day:

Practice training your dog every day. Short, **frequent** training sessions are better than long, infrequent ones.

Train in Short Sessions: Dogs have short attention spans, so keep training sessions short and focused. **Aim** for 10-15 minute sessions and **gradually** increase the **duration** as your dog becomes more **comfortable** with training.

Socialize Your Dog:

Socialize your dog by exposing them to other dogs and people in a controlled **environment**. This will help them learn how to behave around others.

Manage Your Dog's Environment:

Manage your dog's environment to prevent bad behavior. Use a crate or baby gate to keep them from going places they shouldn't, and keep **tempting** items out of reach.

Training should be an enjoyable **experience** for both you and your dog. Use toys and games to make training sessions more **interactive** and engaging for your pet.

Remember, training a pet dog is a lifelong process. Be patient, consistent, and use positive reinforcement to help your dog learn and grow.

4. Language Practice

Complete the sentences using a word from the box.

Or match the words their meaning from the box.

- frequent
- gradually
- comfortable
- manage
- experience
- aim
- duration
- environment
- tempt
- interactive

1) The snow piled up (   ) during the day, turning the schoolyard into a winter wonderland by the time recess came.

2) The librarian displayed new books on the shelf to (   ) the students into exploring different genres and discovering exciting stories.

3) Sally shared her (   ) of visiting the museum over the weekend, describing the fascinating exhibits she saw.

4) The library has a policy of allowing (   ) book checkouts so that students always have something new to read.

5) During reading time, Sarah picked a cozy corner with a soft pillow to make herself (   ) while enjoying her favorite book.

6) During the science experiment, the students had a clear (   ): to observe and record changes in the plants over a two-week period.

7) The (   ) of our field trip to the zoo was four hours, giving us plenty of time to explore and learn about different animals.

8) The teacher used an (   ) whiteboard to make the lesson more engaging, allowing students to participate in solving problems.

9) During the group project, Sarah was chosen as the leader because she knows how to (   ) the team and make sure everyone contributes.

10) During science class, we discussed ways to protect the (   ) and keep our planet clean for future generations.

5. Dog training terminology

Dog training can be a rewarding and fun experience for both you and your furry friend, but it's important to take precautions to ensure the safety of both you and your dog.

Leave it:

A command used to ask the dog to leave an object or item alone.

This command is used to train the dog to leave something alone, such as food or a toy that they may be trying to grab.

Drop it:

A command used to ask the dog to drop an object from its mouth.

Good boy/girl:

A phrase used to praise the dog for good behavior.

This is a phrase that trainers use to praise and reward the dog for good behavior.

❋ No:

A word used to discourage the dog from unwanted behavior.

❋ Wait:

A command used to ask the dog to stop moving and wait for further instructions.

If you're having trouble training your dog, seek professional help from a certified dog trainer.

►Positive reinforcement

Positive reinforcement refers to a training method that focuses on rewarding desired behaviors rather than punishing or correcting unwanted behaviors. It involves using positive stimuli, such as treats, praise, or play, to reinforce behaviors that you want to encourage in your dog.

6. Practical English

Useful expressions for Tourism II

Shopping:

You: How much does this cost?

Shopkeeper: That's $30. Do you want to buy it?

You: Yes, please. Do you accept credit cards?

Shopkeeper: Certainly, we accept all major credit cards.

Emergency(긴급 상황):

You: Excuse me, I need help. Where is the nearest hospital?

Passerby: There's a hospital three blocks away. I can show you.

You: Thank you. I've lost my passport. What should I do?

Police Officer: Go to the nearest embassy. They'll assist you in getting a new one.

Transportation(교통):

You: How much is a ticket to the city center?

Ticket Agent: The ticket is $5. Where are you headed?

You: I need a taxi to the hotel. Is there a taxi stand nearby?

Local: Yes, just outside the terminal.

Everyday Greetings and Conversations(일상적인 인사 및 대화):

You: Hello, how are you?

Local: I'm good, thank you. How about you?

You: I'm great, thanks. Do you speak English?

Local: Yes, I do. How can I help you?

Weather(날씨):

You: What's the weather forecast for today?

Local: It's supposed to be sunny with a high of 25°C.

You: Is it going to rain later?

Local: No, the forecast says it will stay dry.

✿ Inquiring About Hotel Amenities(숙소 이용 문의):

You: Does the hotel provide airport shuttle service?

Hotel Staff: Yes, we do. It runs every hour. Would you like to schedule a pick-up?

✿ Asking for Directions(지도 및 방향 문의):

You: Excuse me, how do I get to [landmark] from here?

Local: You can walk straight for two blocks, then turn left. It's on your right.

Chapter 10

About the manners of dogs I

1. Word Preview

- harmonious
- potential
- accident
- accept
- excessive
- ensure
- drag
- interaction
- encounter
- destructive

• harmonious

The classroom became **harmonious** when everyone worked together to clean up after an art project, putting away materials and organizing the supplies.

① 조화된, 균형 잡힌 ② 화목한, 사이 좋은

• ensure

To **ensure** that everyone has a chance to speak, the teacher encouraged the students to raise their hands and take turns sharing their thoughts during class discussions.

① 을 책임지다, 보장, 보증하다

- **potentially**

The teacher explained that a rainy day could **potentially** change our outdoor recess plans, so we should be prepared for indoor activities.

① 잠재적인, 가능한, 가능성이 있는

- **drag**

During the cleanup time, the teacher reminded the students not to **drag** their chairs across the classroom floor to prevent scratches.

① 끌다, 질질 끌다, 끌어당기다, 끌고 가다

- **accident**

The teacher reminded the students to walk carefully in the hallways to avoid any **accidents** and ensure everyone's safety.

① (돌발) 사고, 재, 재해, 상해

- **interaction**

In the playground, the children engage in friendly **interaction**, playing games and sharing toys to foster a sense of community.

① 상호작용, 컴퓨터에서의 대화

- **accept**

After the game, the students gathered to **accept** their teammates' efforts and celebrate both the victories and the fun they had together

① 받아들이다, 수납하다 ② 수락하다, …에 응하다

- **encounter**

In the library, the students might **encounter** new and exciting books that spark their interest in different genres and subjects.

① (우연히) 만남, 조우

- **excessive**

During the art class, Tim learned that using **excessive** amounts of paint on his canvas created a messy artwork, and he decided to use a more balanced approach.

① 과도한, 과대한, 과다한 ② 지나친, 심한, 엄청난, 무절제한

- **destructive**

The librarian reminded the students not to be **destructive** with library books, encouraging them to handle them gently and return them in good condition.

① 파괴적인, 파괴주의적인, 파멸적인.

2. Useful Expression

① During recess, the students played a **harmonious** game of tag, taking turns and including everyone to ensure that no one felt left out.

② Before the field trip, the teacher reminded the students to **ensure** they had their permission slips signed by their parents for the upcoming visit to the science museum.

③ During the science experiment, we were excited to see how adding baking soda to vinegar could **potentially** create a fizzy reaction.

④ The teacher asked the students not to **drag** their feet in the hallway to keep the floors clean and maintain a safe environment for everyone.

⑤ During the art class, Tim spilled paint on the floor by **accident**, but he quickly cleaned it up with the help of his classmates.

⑥ The science class involves hands-on experiments to encourage **interaction** with various materials and observe different reactions.

⑦ During show-and-tell, the students were excited to **accept** their classmates' presentations and ask questions about the interesting items they brought.

⑧ While playing at recess, the children could **encounter** various challenges, like finding a creative solution to a game or making new friends.

⑨ The teacher reminded the students not to engage in **excessive** talking during quiet reading time, so everyone could focus on their books.

⑩ The teacher explained the importance of taking care of classroom supplies and not engaging in **destructive** behavior, such as scribbling on desks.

3. Reading

Dog manners are important for several reasons, contributing to a positive and **harmonious** relationship between dogs and their owners, as well as **ensuring** the safety and well-being of both the dog and those around them. Here are some key reasons why dog manners are crucial:

Safety:

Well-mannered dogs are less likely to engage in behaviors that can be **potentially** dangerous. For example, a dog with good leash manners is less likely to pull and **drag** their owner, reducing the risk of **accident**s or injuries during walks.

Positive Interactions:

Dogs with good manners are more likely to have positive **interactions** with people, other dogs, and various environments. This contributes to a more enjoyable and stress-free experience for both the dog and their owner.

Public Acceptance:

Dogs with proper manners are more socially **accepted** in public spaces. People are generally more comfortable and welcoming when **encountering** a well-behaved dog, leading to positive experiences for everyone involved.

Reduced Behavioral Issues:

Teaching good manners can help prevent and reduce common behavioral issues such as jumping on people, **excessive** barking, or **destructive** chewing. This, in turn, contributes to a more peaceful and well-adjusted household.

4. Language Practice

Complete the sentences using a word from the box.

Or match the words their meaning from the box.

• harmonious	• ensure
• potentially	• drag
• accidentally	• interaction
• accept	• encounter
• excessive	• destructive

1) The librarian informed us that a (   ) exciting author visit might happen next month, so we should stay tuned for more details.

2) The school assembly was (   ) as students from different grades came together to showcase their talents, creating a joyful and unified atmosphere.

3) The playground monitor asked the students to avoid using (   ) force while playing games to ensure a safe and enjoyable recess for everyone.

4) During the science experiment, the students were careful not to be too rough with the materials to avoid any (   ) impact on the results.

5) To (   ) a fair game, the playground monitor explained the rules to the students and reminded them to follow them while playing soccer during recess.

6) The kids were excited to (   ) their sleds up the hill and then enjoy a thrilling ride down during the snowy recess.

7) During group projects, the teacher encourages positive (   ) among students, where everyone contributes ideas and works together.

8) Kelly apologized to her friend when she bumped into her (   ) while rushing to get in line after recess.

9) The teacher emphasized the importance of kindness, encouraging students to (   ) each other's differences and be inclusive during group activities.

10) During our nature walk, we were fortunate to (   ) a friendly squirrel, and everyone gathered around quietly to observe it.

5. Manners to follow when taking your dog for a walk in the park

- **Keep your pet on a leash:**

Most parks require pets to be on a leash at all times. Even if your pet is well-trained, it's important to keep them on a leash to prevent them from running off and potentially causing harm or getting lost.

- **Bring bags to clean up after your pet:**

Always bring bags to clean up after your pet if they need to go to the bathroom. Properly dispose of the waste in a trash can.

- **Be respectful of others' space:**

Not everyone may be comfortable around pets, so be respectful of other park-goers and keep your pet away from those who may not want to interact with them.

- **Keep your pet under control:**

This includes following basic commands like "sit" and "stay" and not jumping on people. It's also important to keep your pet from running after wildlife or other pets in the park.

- **Be mindful of noise:**

Barking or other loud noises can be disruptive to other park-goers. Try to keep your pet calm and quiet during your time at the park.

- **Respect park rules:**

Be sure to follow any park rules or regulations related to pets. This may include designated pet areas or specific leash requirements.

- **Be prepared:**

Bring water for your pet and yourself, especially on hot days. You should also bring any necessary supplies, such as a first aid kit or medication for your pet.

- **Stay alert:**

Be aware of your surroundings and potential hazards, such as poisonous plants or dangerous animals.

conversation in a hospital

Example 1, Dog's foot pain

Owner: Hi, I think my dog has something in his paw. He's been licking it a lot and seems to be in pain.

Veterinarian: I'm sorry to hear that. Let's take a look. Can you tell me your dog's name and age?

Owner: His name is Charlie, and he's 2 years old.

Veterinarian: Great. Let's have a look at his paw. Oh, I see what's causing the pain. There's a thorn stuck in there. We'll need to remove it.

Owner: Okay. Is it going to hurt him?

Veterinarian: We'll give him some local anesthesia so he doesn't feel anything. It'll just take a few minutes.

Owner: Thank you. How much will this cost?

Veterinarian: It'll be a minor procedure, so it won't cost too much. We'll give you an estimate before we proceed.

Example 2, Dog diet

Owner: Hi, I'm concerned about my dog's weight. She seems to be gaining a lot of weight even though we're feeding her a healthy diet.

Veterinarian: I see. Let's check her weight and talk about her diet. Can you tell me your dog's name and age?

Owner: Her name is Daisy, and she's 5 years old.

Veterinarian: Great. Let's have a look at her weight. Yes, she has gained some weight since her last visit. Let's talk about her diet and exercise routine.

Owner: Okay. What changes can we make to help her lose weight?

Veterinarian: We'll need to adjust her diet and exercise routine. We may need to switch her to a low-calorie diet and increase her exercise. We'll also need to monitor her weight regularly to make sure she's making progress.

Owner: Thank you. How often should we bring her in for check-ups?

Veterinarian: It depends on her progress, but we'll schedule a follow-up appointment in a few weeks to see how she's doing.

6. Practical English

Useful expressions for Tourism II

Ordering Drinks(음료수 주문):

You: I'd like a glass of water, please.

Waiter: Still or sparkling water?

You: Still water is fine, thank you.

Getting Travel Tips(여행 팁 얻기):

You: Any recommendations for must-see places in the city?

Local: You should visit [attraction] and try the local cuisine at [restaurant].

Extending Check-out Time(체크아웃 시간 연장):

You: Is it possible to extend my check-out time to 1 PM?

Hotel Staff: Yes, we can arrange a late check-out for you.

Exploring the City(도시 탐험):

You: What's the best way to explore the city on foot?

Local: You can take a walking tour or use a map to discover the main attractions.

Currency Exchange(화폐 교환):

You: Where can I exchange my currency to local currency?

Bank Clerk: The nearest currency exchange is at the shopping mall, just two blocks away.

Inquiring about Internet(인터넷 문의):

You: Is there Wi-Fi available in the hotel?

Hotel Staff: Yes, we provide complimentary Wi-Fi. The password is on the information card in your room.

Negotiating in a Shop(상점에서 흥정):

You: Is the price negotiable for this item?

Shopkeeper: We can offer a discount if you pay in cash.

Chapter 11

About the manners of dogs Ⅱ

1. Word Preview

- respond
- expectation
- include
- foundation
- compliance
- convey
- access
- development
- legal
- regulation

• respond

When the fire alarm sounded, the students knew to **respond** quickly and line up quietly to exit the building.

① 응답하다, 대답하다, 응(수)하다, 반응하다

• convey

In our writing assignment, we were asked to choose descriptive words to **convey** the feelings of the main character in the story.

① 나르다, 운반(운송)하다

- **expectation**

The school assembly had the **expectation** that students would show respect by sitting quietly and listening to the guest speaker.

① 예상, 예기; 기대

- **access**

The computer lab provides students with **access** to educational games and online resources to enhance their learning experience.

① 접근 근접

- **include**

The teacher encouraged students to **include** specific details in their writing to make their stories more interesting and engaging for the readers.

① 포함하다

- **development**

The teacher explained that daily reading helps with language **development**, expanding our vocabulary and comprehension skills.

① 발달, 발전, 발육, 성장

- **foundation**

During the art class, we practiced drawing shapes and lines as the **foundation** for creating more detailed and intricate artworks later on.

① 창설, 창립, 건립

- **legal**

During the safety lesson, the students learned about the **legal** requirements for wearing helmets while riding bikes to prevent accidents.

① 법률(상)의, 법률에 관한

- **compliance**

During the fire drill, the teacher ensured that everyone moved quickly and quietly in **compliance** with the safety procedures.

① 승낙, 응낙 ② 고분고분함, 굴종

- **regulation**

The school has a **regulation** stating that students must wear uniforms, ensuring a neat and consistent appearance.

① 규칙, 규정, 법규, 조례

2. Useful Expression

① During the show-and-tell, each student had the chance to present their item, and the classmates were encouraged to **respond** by asking questions or sharing their thoughts.

② The teacher used a map to **convey** the concept of distance and location, helping the students understand the geography lesson better.

③ During the spelling test, the students had the **expectation** to spell the words correctly based on their weekly practice.

④ The teacher reminded the students to respect each other's privacy and not **access** someone else's belongings without permission.

⑤ During recess, the children made sure to **include** everyone in their game, so no one felt left out or lonely.

⑥ During the art project, the students focused on the creative **development** of their ideas, turning simple sketches into colorful and imaginative drawings.

⑦ The teacher explained that understanding the rules of addition and subtraction is the **foundation** for solving more complex math problems in the future.

⑧ The librarian reminded the students that it is not **legal** to damage or deface library books, and they should handle them with care.

⑨ he librarian appreciated the students' **compliance** with library rules, such as returning books on time and maintaining a quiet atmosphere for reading.

⑩ During the science experiment, the students followed the **regulation** of wearing safety goggles to protect their eyes from any potential harm.

3. Reading

Here are some key reasons why dog manners are crucial:

Improved Bond:

Training and reinforcing good manners create a stronger bond between the dog and the owner. Dogs that understand and **respond** to commands are more likely to feel **secure** and confident in their relationship with their human companions.

Enhanced Communication:

Good manners provide a means of communication between the dog and their owner. Commands and cues help **convey expectations**, making it easier for the dog to understand what is required of them in different situations.

Public Access:

Dogs with good manners are more likely to be welcomed in various public spaces, including parks, cafes, and stores. This makes it easier for owners to **include** their dogs in daily activities and outings.

Prevention of Behavioral Problems:

Establishing good manners early in a dog's life can prevent the **development** of more serious behavioral problems in the future. Consistent training and reinforcement create a **foundation** for positive behavior.

Stress Reduction:

Dogs that know what is expected of them and are well-socialized experience less stress in new or challenging situations. This leads to a more relaxed and happy dog.

Legal Compliance:

In many places, there are legal requirements for dog owners to have control over their pets in public spaces. Ensuring good manners in dogs helps owners comply with local laws and **regulations**.

4. Language Practice

Complete the sentences using a word from the box.

Or match the words their meaning from the box.

• respond	• convey
• expectation	• access
• include	• development
• foundation	• legal
• compliance	• regulation

1) In science class, we learned about the life cycle of a butterfly and how it undergoes different stages of (   ).

2) Learning the alphabet and basic counting in kindergarten is crucial for building a strong (   ) in language and math skills.

3) The teacher asked the students to raise their hands and wait patiently to (   ) to questions during the class discussion.

4) During the art class, the students used various colors and shapes to (   ) their emotions and ideas in their paintings.

5) The students were excited to (   ) the new library books that the librarian had just added to the shelves.

6) The students were praised for their (   ) with the school's recycling program, as they consistently separated recyclables from other waste.

7) The teacher set clear (   ) for behavior in the classroom, reminding students to listen attentively and raise their hands before speaking.

8) In the group project, each student had a chance to (   ) their ideas, creating a collaborative and diverse final presentation.

9) The teacher explained the (   ) for using indoor voices in the library to maintain a quiet and focused atmosphere for reading.

10) The teacher explained that it is not (   ) to copy someone else's homework, as it is a form of cheating.

5. Dog manners to keep in public places

- Follow leash laws: In many public places, pets are required to be on a leash. Make sure you follow these laws and keep your pet on a leash at all times.

- Clean up after your pet: Always bring bags to pick up after your pet, whether it's in a park or on a sidewalk. Properly dispose of the waste in a trash can.

- Avoid off-limit areas: Respect signs that prohibit pets from certain areas, such as playgrounds or public pools.

- Keep your pet under control: Ensure that your pet is well-behaved and under your control. Don't let them jump on people, pull on their leash, or cause any disturbances.

- Ask for permission: If you want to bring your pet to a public establishment like a restaurant or store, always ask for permission beforehand. Not all places allow pets, so it's important to respect their rules.

- Be mindful of others: Remember that not everyone is comfortable around pets or may have allergies. Always be considerate of others and keep your pet away from those who may not want to interact with them.

conversation at a dog salon

Example 1, Bath and brush-out

Hairdresser: Hi there! Welcome to our pet grooming salon. What can we help you with today?

Customer: Hi, I have a Golden Retriever that needs a bath and brush-out. He's been shedding a lot lately and needs some help with that.

Hairdresser: Sure thing. We can definitely give him a bath and brush-out to help with his shedding. Does he have any skin or coat issues we should know about?

Customer: No, he's healthy and just needs a good cleaning.

Hairdresser: Great. We'll give him a nice bath, use a conditioning treatment to help with his coat, and do a thorough brush-out to remove any loose fur. Is there anything else you'd like us to do?

Customer: No, that's all for now. Thank you.

Example 2, Nail trim

Hairdresser: Hi there! How can we help you and your pet today?

Customer: Hi, I have a dog that needs her nails trimmed. They're getting pretty long.

Hairdresser: Sure thing. We can definitely trim her nails. Would you like us to do anything else, like a bath or a brush-out?

Customer: No, just the nail trim for now.

Hairdresser: Okay, we'll take good care of her and make sure she's comfortable throughout the process.

6. Practical English

Useful expressions for symptoms in hospitals

Pain(통증):

"아프다" (It hurts.)

"이곳이 아파요" (It hurts here.)

"심한 통증이 있어서 왔어요" (I came because of severe pain.)

Fever(열):

"열이 나서 몸이 뜨거워져요" (I have a fever and my body feels hot.)

"열이 몇 도 나와요?" (What is my temperature?)

Difficulty Breathing(호흡곤란):

"숨쉬기가 힘들어졌어요" (I'm having difficulty breathing.)

"가슴이 답답하게 느껴져요" (I feel tightness in my chest.)

Vomiting(구토):

“구토가 나와서 걱정돼요” (I'm worried because I'm vomiting.)

“식사 후에 구토가 자주 일어나요” (I vomit frequently after meals.)

Diarrhea or Constipation(설사 또는 변비):

“설사가 자주 나와요” (I have frequent diarrhea.)

“변비로 고생하고 있어요” (I'm suffering from constipation.)

Headache(두통):

“머리가 아파서 힘들어요” (I have a headache and it's difficult.)

“머리가 계속 아파요” (I have a persistent headache.)

Fatigue(피로감):

“체력이 많이 떨어져서 피곤해요” (I'm tired because my energy is low.)

“하루 종일 피로감이 있어요” (I feel fatigue all day.)

Malaise(미열):

"몸이 어지러워요" (I feel dizzy.)

"몸 전체가 힘들어져서 왔어요" (I came because my whole body feels weak.)

Abdominal Pain with Vomiting or Diarrhea(구토나 설사와 함께한 복통):

"복부가 아파서 병원에 왔어요" (I came to the hospital because my abdomen hurts.)

"구토와 함께 복통이 있어요" (I have abdominal pain along with vomiting.)

Reference

김옥진(2020), 인간과 동물, 동일출판사

박효진 외(2023), 응용동물훈련, 동문사

장정은(2022), 반려견스타일리스트, 동문사

최농락 외(2022), Understanding The companion animal industry, 동문사

김옥진 외(2020), Animal behavior counseling, 동일출판사

이승현(2020), KKF 훈련사 자격교재, 한국애견연맹

이해연 외(2016), 트리머 매뉴얼, 한국애견연맹

김병부 외(2020), 반려동물행동교정, 한국애견연맹

최재헌 외(2022), 애견학개론, KPETEDU

Holiday inn Manual.

Hyatt Hotel Manual.

Yandon Ju, Robert gallagher(2018), Seromi

https://en.wikipedia.org/wiki/Akita_(dog)

https://huffpost.com›entry 'Groundbreaking' Trial Will Test Cancer-Sniffing Dogs By Dominique Mosbergen Sep 7, 2015

www.reuters.com›article

https://en.wikipedia.org/wiki/Rin_Tin_Tin

https://en.wikipedia.org/wiki/Smoky_(dog)

https://en.wikipedia.org/wiki/Siberian_Husky

https://en.wikipedia.org/wiki/Chips_(dog)

저자소개

이원봉

대덕대학교 반려동물과
대덕대학교 호텔외식서비스과
세종대학교 경영학박사
Florida International University, School of Hospitality Management(석사)

반려동물 기초 생활영어

초판 1쇄 인쇄 / 2024년 1월 20일
초판 1쇄 발행 / 2024년 1월 25일

저 자 / 이 원 봉
발행인 / 이 중 수
발행처 / **동 문 사**

서울특별시 서대문구 홍제원 1길 12
(홍제동 137-8)
Tel: 02)736-3718(대), 736-3710, 3720
Fax: 02)736-3719
등록번호: 1974.04.27. 제9-17호
가격: 16,000원

ISBN: 979-11-6328-574-8(93740)
E-mail: dong736@naver.com
www.dongmunsa.com